The Nibble Theory
and
The Kernel of Power

A Book About Leadership,
Self-empowerment and Personal Growth

Kaleel Jamison

Paulist Press, ⌇ **New York/Ramsey**

Acknowledgements:
Sandra Smythe
Maryann MacDonald
Frederick A. Miller
Nancy Brown
Lourice Fattaleh
Kay Pinkvoss
George Dershimer
Patricia Volk
Pat Ikeda
All of the foregoing have given blood in this enterprise.

Excerpt from "Feet Live Their Own Life," from *The Best of Simple*, by Langston Hughes (Hill and Wang, a division of Farrar, Straus and Giroux, Inc., 1961). Reprinted by permission in *The American Tradition*, edited by Bradley et al. (Grosset & Dunlap, Inc.: Volume II, pp. 1460 ff.).

Excerpt from "Harlem" copyright 1951 by Langston Hughes, is from *The Panther and the Lash* by Langston Hughes, and is used by permission of Alfred A. Knopf, Inc. and Harold Ober Associates.

Library of Congress
Catalog Card Number: 83-63112

ISBN: 0-8091-0354-0

Published by Paulist Press
545 Island Road, Ramsey, N.J. 07446

Printed and bound in the
United States of America

Contents

To Bill:
Who has lovingly helped me grow.

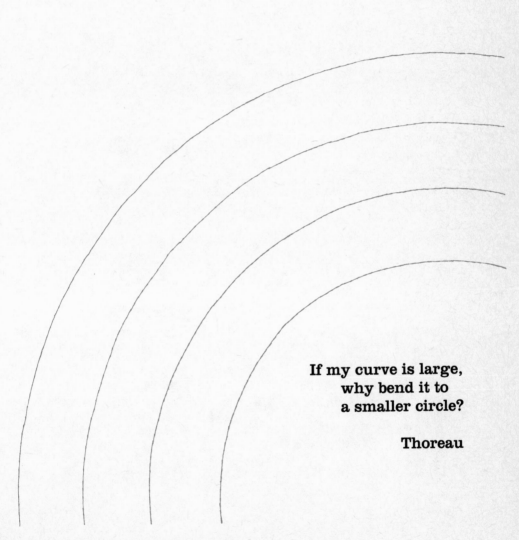

If my curve is large,
why bend it to
a smaller circle?

Thoreau

The Nibble Theory

The Theory

This book is about growth—yours, mine, children's, co-workers', everybody's.

It is about how all of us can grow—to be the very best and most powerful persons we can imagine, as we were meant to be.

The idea is called "the nibble theory," but that name describes what *not* to do.

The technique for growth is simple, but it is *not* easy.

This is not a book about control. It's a book about self-empowerment. And growth. And celebration—of self and the joy of contributing to the growth of others.

Some call this theory generous; some call it productive. I call it a way of living.

This way of living works like a candle. When you give away some of the light from the candle, by lighting another person's candle, there isn't *less* light because you've given some away—there's more. That works with love too. And that works with this growth theory.

When *everybody* grows, there isn't less of *anybody;* there's more of—and for—everybody.

Since what we're talking about is personal growth for so many kinds of people, in so many ways, it might simplify matters to talk about growth by using a symbol.

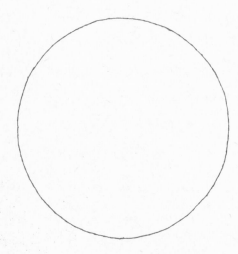

So let's agree, shall we, that we'll let a circle stand for a person. And we will be able to diagram growth, and relative position, and other things we want to talk about more easily.

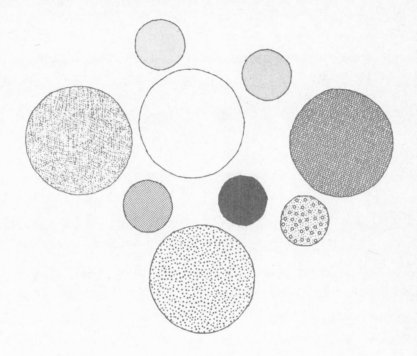

We all live in groups, all kinds of groups: families, schools, offices, factories, clubs, social circles. And within all of these groups we each occupy a position and have influence in relation to the other members of the group.

Some are big circles—leaders, movers, shakers, initiators, independent thinkers.

Some are smaller circles—second in command, responders, reactors, a little less powerful.

Some are small circles indeed—retiring, followers, hesitators, even shy non-contributors.

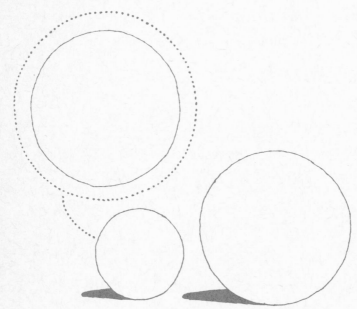

Everybody could be big—theoretically. But some choose to be small. Some would like to be bigger but don't know how. Some never think of themselves as able to be bigger.

Some would like to be bigger but get themselves all bent out of shape trying—and never get bigger, just all out of shape.

But everybody wants to grow. It's a drive from the time we are born. And even when we are, as we say, "grown," physically, we still want to grow—in knowledge, and power, and importance in the human groups we belong to.

It's not *always* true that bigger is better, but in this case growing bigger *is* better.

There's nothing wrong with this wish to grow. The human organism is designed to grow toward health. It's healthy to want to grow —just as the physical drive to grow is healthy and irresistible.

How we grow is the thing. Many people go about it all wrong.

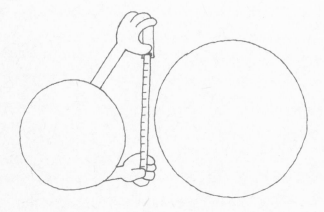

When two circles meet, or when they have a chance to sit down and look at each other, they size each other up. They come to know very soon who is big and who is small.

And then the relationship begins.

Two things can happen: the small circle can begin to get bigger —react as the independent, competent, contributing being he or she is.

Or the nibbling can begin.

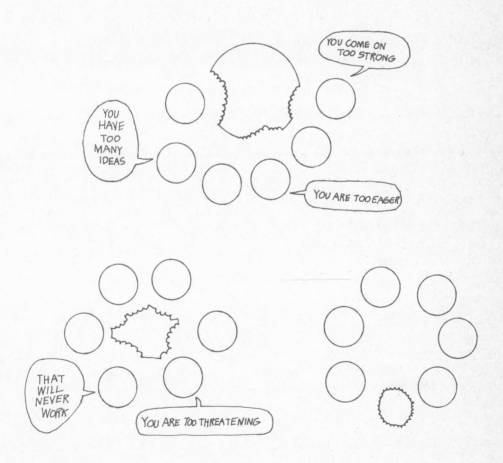

Nibbling is a common occurrence. Most people do nibble, unless they have learned to do something else. There's a better way to grow. We'll talk about that later.

Nibbles are easy to recognize, once you've seen a few:

You ask too may questions.

You always give your ideas first.

You're too direct.
You're too nice.
You're too concerned about people.

You work too hard.
You use too many big words.
You're too frank.
You're too friendly.
You're too helpful.

You're too emotional.
You're too sensitive.
You're too serious.

Caution: Some of these *could* be legitimate invitations to grow. How do you tell the difference? A nibble asks you to make yourself less powerful. An invitation to grow says: keep the power and size you have; and add more skills to make you a bigger circle.

SANDY, YOU TALK TOO MUCH. YOU SHOULD TALK LESS SO LEE CAN TALK MORE.

A NIBBLE

WHEN YOU TALK, SANDY, ALL OF YOUR COMMENTS ARE CLEAR AND USEFUL. AFTER YOU HAVE SPOKEN, ASK WHAT IDEAS LEE HAS TO OFFER.

GROWTH INVITATION

Many people look at themselves, and they look at others, and they think that the way to get bigger themselves is to get others down to size, make others smaller. So they start to nibble.

11

This activity is not restricted to small circles' nibbling of big circles. Sometimes big circles nibble to keep small circles small—and in their place.

"That's a dumb idea." Or some subtler form of this, like: "I don't think we can do that. It's been tried before and it didn't work."

Or: "We've always done it this way."

"This is not really your field, is it?"

"What do you really know about it?"

TRANSLATION: DON'T CHANGE (GROW).
I LIKE YOU JUST THE WAY YOU ARE
(SMALLER THAN ME).

Or a simple refusal to consider your idea, or the ignoring of your comment.

"Mmn hmnnn." [With a vague, distracted air that says clearly, "I'm not listening."]

"Tell you what. Why don't you just stick to what you have to do, and we'll handle this." [Translation: Mind your own business. We're not letting you in on the interesting stuff—and you can't make us.]

All this is aggravating. And diminishing. And embarrassing. And off-putting. Worst of all, it's non-productive, for the group and for the people in it. Because if everybody grows to be as big as possible, to realize the talents and strengths he or she has, everybody benefits.

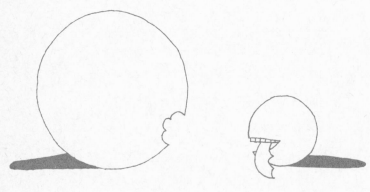

CLOSE-UP OF A NIBBLE

People nibble for all kinds of reasons. For one thing, nibbling is less risky and less painful than growing. Nibbling hurts you. Nibbling is done to you. Growing *I* have to do—and that's not easy.

The kinds of nibbles we have talked about are open—overt nibbles. There are also covert nibbles, and they can be even more deadly in putting the quietus on somebody else's growth than the open ones.

I've been in groups, for instance, that have scotched the growth of new members by doing nothing. Just that. Nothing. How can doing nothing be a nibble? Well, suppose a newcomer suggests something that is a perfectly good idea but not the kind of thing accepted in that community. By *not* telling newcomers when they are violating the norms of the group, the group's established members can nibble the new people down and make their growth and acceptance in that group impossible. In fact, whenever members of a group know that what new members are about to do will leave them out on a limb and then withhold the information, that's a nibble.

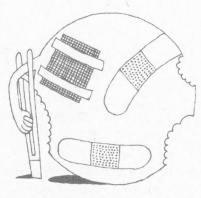

A BADLY NIBBLED CIRCLE

And people permit themselves to be nibbled for all sorts of reasons. If, for instance, I'm a big circle and you nibble at me, I *can* make myself smaller.

And because I have tried to please you, I *think* we will be friends. But when my *need* to grow asserts itself again, when I am—as I inevitably will be—searching again to find a way to make myself a bigger circle—a contributing, responsible member of the group—I may feel the nibble keenly and begin to dislike myself, because I feel betrayed. By whom? *By me.*

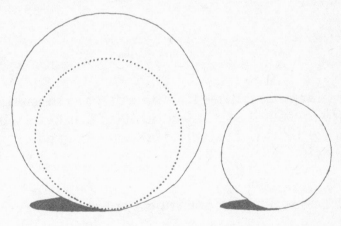

COMFORT: I MAKE MYSELF SMALLER, SO YOU WILL BE COMFORTABLE. I WANT YOU TO LIKE ME.

SELF-BETRAYAL

The times in my life when I feel the worst are those times when I've not been true to myself—have not said what I think, feel, believe. That's the time when I've betrayed myself, diminished my energy by confining my growth to keep myself small.

Can you recall a time when you betrayed yourself?

How did you feel?

Do you know why you betrayed yourself?

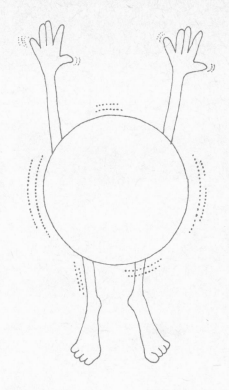

Growing—Yourself

There is, on the other hand, another way. There's room, and time, and the *right* for both of us to grow—and be bigger circles. *Everybody* can be bigger, without anybody having to be smaller. Remember, power—like energy, and light, and love—can be infinitely expanded.

Why Grow?

Silly question? Not at all. More people than you think are afraid to grow. Especially when there is a risk involved—and there is almost always a risk of some kind. "I might," after all, "get nibbled myself." Yes, you might. But you might also manage to deflect the nibble and find yourself a bigger circle—feeling good about yourself.

One unspoken fear is the idea that if you become personally power-ful, you will become isolated. We all live with the fear that if we grow bigger than others, we will be excluded. The only way, we think, to stay included in the group, to stay warm and accepted, is to remain small. This is a phenomenon that happens more often than you might suppose in business. And in other parts of life as well.

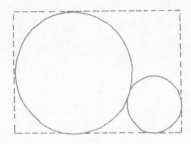

FEAR:
IF I LET YOU GROW
THERE WON'T BE ENOUGH
SPACE FOR ME TO BE BIG.

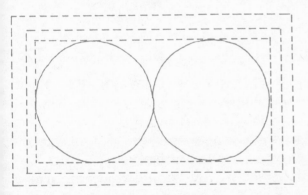

TRUTH:
THERE ARE **NO** BOUNDARIES.

People engage in self-limiting behavior, because they fear isolation if they advance. Many children in school don't want to appear smarter than others. Some girls and women still think that they can't afford to appear as smart or as capable as boys or men if boys and men are to find them attractive.

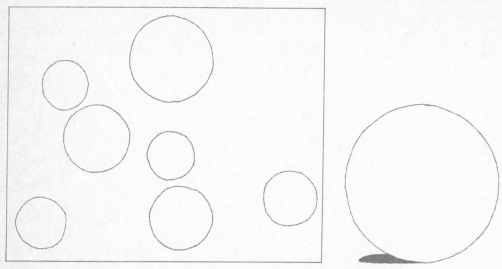

FEAR: IF I AM BIG YOU WON'T INCLUDE ME.

But the best thing that can happen is for a big circle to hold its head up high and know that there are times when a big circle will be lonely. But when that happens, that circle can do several things:

- It can look for other big circles to keep it company.
- It can remember that *it* is still growing and look for bigger circles to be with—in a place where growth is encouraged.
- It can be a model and encourage smaller circles to grow.

Self-Effacement Isn't a Good Idea

It must be one of those funny misinterpretations of a religious teaching in our culture—something like the idea that pride is one of the deadly sins. But somehow we have got that idea all out of shape—and ourselves along with it. *I* believe that the basic message religion means to teach us is to be most fully ourselves, to tap into the God-like being in us.

Power is not bad unless it is wrongly used. Power can be used for good.

Everybody is a big circle in some part of her or his world. Even extreme cases of small circles are big circles somewhere, with somebody. And everybody needs to be a big circle somewhere. This may account for why some people kick their dogs.

Here's what I say to you. Everything I tell you comes out of my own experience. Everything I understand, I understand because once I did it all wrong and had to find a better way. To women, I say: I have done it all—lost my way, lost my identity, clung to my husband, and had to find my way again—and again. To all circles, I say: Don't be impatient with yourself. Growing takes time and help and support. And faith.

Remember back to a time when you risked and it worked. Each time I face the difficulties of a new dilemma, I remind myself that everything I know and have learned has come because of a hard experience that I walked *through*—not away from. Then, I got through it—learned from the experience—and now I can celebrate what it showed me.

Everyone wants personal power. I do. Oh yes, you do too. And there's nothing wrong with wanting that. That's only part of wanting to be as good as you can be.

Nor do I think that people, once empowered, will abuse their power. Only small circles, who *feel* small and frustrated about it, have to kick their dogs. Power itself is a neutral force. It can be used for good or for ill. But feeling comfortable with it, feeling competent about what you do will free you from the need to prove anything at all. You decide—and you're perfectly qualified to do so—how you will use your power. You can learn—if you don't already know—how to be reflective, to think about how your power affects others. And when you think about that, you can use it for good purposes—to help others grow, and to grow yourself even further.

Nobody likes to feel *without* power. Children have very little power. Maybe that's why there's a bully on every block. Children have to spend a long time getting their relationships to each other adjusted, and they don't have much experience to help them.

And we tell them, "Be nice." That's fine, but they need to know—as do we all—how to be nice and still be true to themselves and not restrict their own sense of power.

We all need to feel that we matter in our worlds, that people notice us and take us seriously. It's only when we don't feel that way that we don't treat others right. That's when our power can become abusive.

You can be a big circle. It's possible. It's okay. It's desirable. It's what you should do. You should grow. But there is a right way and a wrong way. The wrong way is to nibble—or to let yourself be nibbled.

How to Grow

Decide you're going to. Decide that it's the right thing for you to do. Decide that your growth won't limit the growth of others.

Decide that you're not going to be nibbled. Decide that you're not going to nibble anyone else.

Decide that you want to be the biggest circle you can be.

The best way to experience growth is to be in a group where there is plenty of room for many big circles. And where your growth doesn't have to make others in the group smaller. Some people simply stumble on such an experience. I did. I stumbled into a group where I was treated as if I were a big circle. So I became one. I grew, because other big circles helped me to grow. They encouraged me to grow, but they didn't do it for me.

How did they help me? Well, they didn't let their roles—or mine —get in the way. They took my ideas seriously, although—perhaps —some of those weren't good, or very developed just then. But instead of knocking my ideas, they listened. They built on the things I said—however haltingly I said them. They helped me to see how to make my ideas better, and they told me their experiences. They saw different ideas as ways to discover more and see new solutions to a problem.

The best way to grow is with a group of people who are generous and who are themselves big circles. I'm glad that's the way it happened to me. But that doesn't always happen. Sometimes other big circles in a group assume that there is only room for one—or two—big circles. They think what many people think—that if somebody grows bigger, others must be smaller. That's not true. But you have to experience growth to know that.

Growth is sometimes taking place even when it isn't obvious. Every human being has boundaries. These invisible lines that contain our selves sometimes need to have open gates—open to stimulus and experience. But sometimes they need to be closed, to shield the renewal and growth taking place inside. Both conditions contribute to growth. Sometimes, when I am ready to be open, I can take all the stimuli I can get. I read—newspapers, books, anything I can lay my hands on. I discuss, I see my friends. I go out. I meet new people, make new friends. I seek out more material to think about and feel about. I am active and moving in an outward directed growth.

But sometimes, when my processing apparatus is fully loaded, I have to close off my boundaries to prevent overload. So I limit my telephone calls. I stop reading the paper. I don't look at television. I don't read. Those seem to be the times when I consolidate my earlier gains, when I heal my wounds, when I balance my inner self. These seem to me as much growth periods as the more outgoing times. Nearly every plant has a period of dormancy that is necessary to its further growth. And so, I suspect, do most human beings.

Both conditions—open and closed—contribute to growth.

Each condition, however, has to be balanced by the other. My friend Helen has always been an open, outgoing woman. She is very beautiful, and is capable and competent at her job. But a frightening experience in her personal life had caused her to close herself off so completely that she was not able to grow in her work or to deal with the personal problem. A respected colleague insisted that she tell a few of her trusted friends she worked with what was happening to her. It was hard for her to confide in these people, but when she did she got such sincere caring and support that she was able to carry on with her work life and cope with the outside situation. They understood. Similar things had happened to them. She no longer thought she was the *only* one who had felt as she did. But it was necessary for her to open her boundaries and get the support she needed from others before she could continue her own growth.

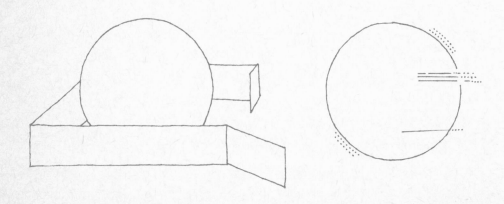

Sometimes we have to open our boundaries. Sometimes they have to be closed. Always we have to be willing to risk in order to grow.

Understand that you will have growing pains. Understand that there will be times when saying "yes" to yourself and your need to grow may include saying "no" to what someone else has in mind for you.

Be brave. Every time you do this, it gets easier. You don't have to be unpleasant or inconsiderate. You just have to decide whether you're being nibbled or whether the demand being made on you might be legitimate and a growth challenge in itself. It helps to understand what's happening. And even to say it.

BE BRAVE!

Understand, too, that people grow in different ways—some openly, some noisily, some quietly. Be compassionate about the growth of others. But do not expect others to grow in your image.

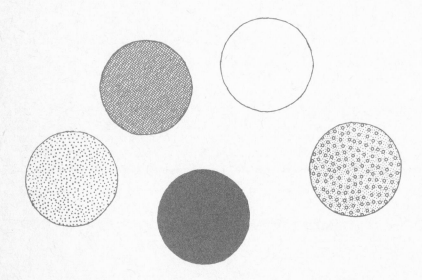

This is a real trap if you are already a big circle, or if you've already done some of your own growing. Don't make the mistake of saying: "She's not (he's not) growing the way I have." Be sensitive to the patterns of behavior in others, and try to see what others are striving to achieve.

Most people are usually doing the best they can. Everything people do is being done out of their own experience. That's useful for me to remember when I'm encouraging somebody else to grow. If I *advise* somebody else, I have to remember that I am advising out of my own experience and telling a method that I have found useful. When I tell what I think is the very best way to handle something, however, I *may* miss what is happening to you. If I am too intent on telling you *my* experience, or too intent on doing what *I* think best, I may miss what you are telling me about your experience and your best way.

So when a parent—or teacher—or manager is showing someone how to accomplish something, it is easy to be focused on "the right way." A "gift of knowledge and experience" is the intent. But the large circle must not forget that only as small circles incorporate the given knowledge with their own best way of doing things do they grow in wisdom and *become* larger circles.

The human potential for growth is not limited. Mine isn't. And yours isn't.

It is right and proper for you to grow, for you to continue to become the biggest circle you can be. That doesn't mean that you will have to nibble anybody else, to make somebody else smaller, so that you can be bigger. It doesn't mean that you have to submit to being nibbled. It does mean that when you are bigger you can help others to be bigger too.

My father came to this country as a Lebanese immigrant. When he arrived, he had no money and no English. What gave him the courage to do that has always been one of my favorite stories. In the small village where Papa grew up an orphan—he and his older brother responsible for a younger sister—there was a man named Charlie Tweel. Charlie Tweel had gone to America and had made enough money to come back to visit his home village. Papa always told us as we were growing up that that visit from Charlie Tweel is what gave him the courage to strike out for America. He said, "I decided that if an ordinary man like Charlie Tweel could do it, so could I." So at sixteen Papa and his cousin set out for America. They had a hundred dollars, high hopes, and not much information. Afraid that they would not be allowed in at Ellis Island, because they couldn't speak English, they detoured through Mexico, where they found a friendly border guard who helped them into the promised land. Papa made his way to Minnesota, where he worked as a farm hand, and then to West Virginia to a settlement of Lebanese people and finally founded the small confectionary business that nurtured all of us. Charlie Tweel's success made him a big circle model for my father. Something in Papa identified with the part of Charlie that had taken the risk, and Papa found the courage to follow his own destiny.

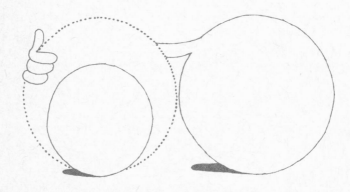

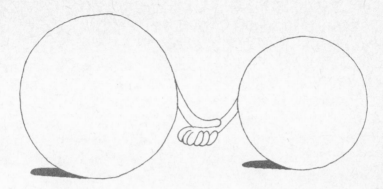

Helping Others To Grow

Power is neutral. You can handle it for good or for harm. And you can help others to acquire it properly and use it properly, by how you treat them. How you treat others who are trying to grow is very important.

You can help to set the environment—in any group that you're in—that will help everybody to grow.

You can enter into—and encourage—the kind of conflict that educates—that is productive.

I do not think that happiness is never to have pain. And it's not my goal to make people comfortable. It *is* my goal to offer the kind of straight talk to other people that produces growth—and may bring with it temporary discomfort.

What a good teacher does, and what you too can do, to help others grow is this: Look—look hard—for the small, perhaps awkward, groping, weak attempt to grow. It is often almost covered over with something else ridiculous, or embarrassing. But to learn, we all have to make a first movement—however wide of the mark. Only by doing, and correcting, and doing again do we zero in on the target. It is not your responsibility to do the practicing for the other person, but it is your—perhaps sacred, human—responsibility to respect that first, tentative movement, to find in it what is right—even if that is only the will to make the movement—and to nurture that so that the next attempt is better. You do that by making an honest, appreciative, human reaction.

We all carry burdens with us that others don't suspect. And those burdens color how we feel and how we think—and affect whether or not we are able to risk and grow.

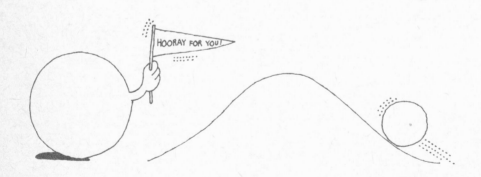

Further, because growth always requires risk, it also always causes us to become vulnerable. And when we are vulnerable, we are easy targets for nibblers—usually on just those areas where, because of old experiences, we are most sensitive. When you're in a group where you sense that people are trying to grow, it is important to be sensitive, and alert, and respectful, because it is easy to hit an exposed nerve. You never know when a careless remark—or an out and out nibble—will tap into an early rejection and stop the new growth in its tracks.

A friend of mine who is a high school teacher once told me about an experience she had in her classroom—an experience that was to leave her, she says, more alert for the rest of her life. One hot, sultry day near the end of the term, class wasn't going well. She felt pressed to finish the day's material. The class was restless, and progress was slow. At the back of the room were three girls who were being particularly disturbing. They were whispering and writing notes and inattentive, even when her stern glances were noticed. Finally, she was exasperated, and it was on the tip of her tongue to say, "I would suggest that you leave this class unless you can manage to pay attention and not disturb the rest of us." Something in the expression of one of the girls stopped her, however, and she went on with the class without saying anything. When class was over, she set to collecting her materials to move on to the next class. She looked up to see the three girls waiting to talk to her. "Mrs. Howell," said one, "we want to apologize for not paying much attention in class. You see, Margaret just had a telephone call before we came in: our best friend died this morning." For months these girls had been carrying the burden of the impending death of their friend, Lisa—a fifteen-year-old who had leukemia. They had valiantly—perhaps numbly—come to class in spite of their grief and bewilderment, but they hadn't been able to concentrate on English literature. My friend says she shudders when she thinks what her own insensitive comment might have added to the burden they were already carrying. She says she has never forgotten that day whenever she is inclined to act without a moment's pause to inquire.

Take time to listen—and to sense—what is happening to the other person. You may *feel* impatient with what is happening. But find out what it is about. Let me repeat that. It's worth repeating. Find out what behavior is about. Take the extra time. The more I watch human beings, the more I understand the need to bide my time and allow the full course of growth to come about. When growth begins, a person is often "raggedy" and unskilled. Joan, who is a white woman, has been a small circle with other people. Even though she is good at her job, she's not comfortable talking in groups. At work she was asked by Miriam, a black woman manager, for some straight answers about how Miriam had presented a special report. Joan was not honest with Miriam. In fact, Joan said that Miriam had "done well." But that was *not* what Joan thought. She thought Miriam needed to improve. Later Joan admitted that she hadn't been honest because she thought that a black person would be angry to receive criticism from a white person. Miriam was angry and hurt by Joan's failure to be honest with her. Miriam had her own painful past experiences with white people, but she had specifically asked Joan for her opinion and wanted an honest answer. When Joan realized and admitted what she had done, she began to grow. It would take time and practice with being honest with black people for Joan to become a larger circle. But the growth *was already taking* place. It just hadn't yet gone as far as it would eventually go to become a significant growth experience for Joan. Miriam thought that straight criticism would have been helpful to her. In her hurt and carrying the burden of her past experiences, it was hard for Miriam to see that Joan had already begun to grow. It takes practice—and understanding—to let the growth process take place, through all its raggedy stages.

The Kernel of Power

The Theory

And now we come to the hardest part. This is the simplest part of the theory—and the best—but it is by no means the easiest to do.

This is a process toward understanding yourself, respecting yourself, and empowering yourself.

Remember, when you're struggling through this, that what is at stake is *you*—what you are now, and what you can grow to be.

I once knew a wise man—a teacher of very young children. Under his supervision, children blossomed. Children who couldn't do math could do math. Youngsters who couldn't play sports could play sports. He was one of those magical people who show you what you can do that you never thought you could do. He used to say that we would never ask a duck to climb a tree—a duck's not equipped to do that with webbed feet.

But the duck swims superbly.
We wouldn't ask a donkey to dance,
but a donkey is strong and sure-footed.
It can pull heavy loads and go
where other animals can't go.

This man—this immensely gifted teacher—knew that it was only necessary to help each child to discover the one thing that he or she *could* do well. And with that as a pivot, with that to give them confidence and a feeling of self-worth, they could do other things—things they never thought they could do. Under his tutelage, children grew in all directions and became happy, busy, eager, contributing human beings. The teacher was himself a very big circle, with a very big reputation. But he never got in the way of the children's growth.

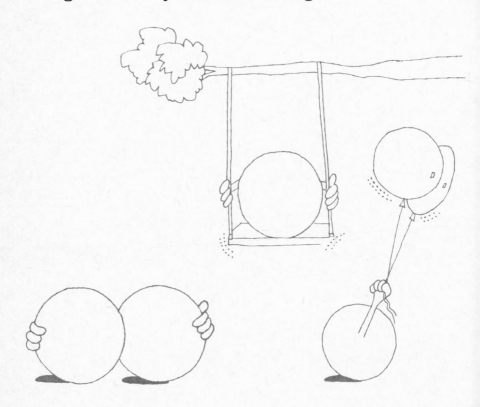

Discovering your kernel of power is something like what he did with children. It works this way.

You *do* have power. Yes you do. It comes from the very center of yourself—your kernel—the part of you that is unique.

On the one hand, as human beings we are alike in many fundamental ways. We all share certain

- physical needs;
- feelings of grief at death;
- a wish to love and be loved;
- care and concern for our children.

Carl Rogers said: "What's most personal is universal."

On the other hand, like snowflakes, no two people are truly alike. You are unique, and I am unique. And so is every other being ever born or yet to be born.

That's an awesome paradox. And a great mystery.

You must discover what it is that you brought into this world with your Self—your unique Self—that nobody else has.

As Langston Hughes' character, Simple, says "Everything I do is connected up with my past life . . . from my mother's milk to this glass of beer, everything is connected up."

Simple's right. Everything that has ever happened to you in your life is valuable and connected to everything else that you do and think and feel forever. That makes you unique. You can't change the past —and that's okay. That frees you to choose—this way or that and change, this way or that, what happens to you. That's the way you've grown, that's the shape you've grown into from your past experiences. That's the shape you are. With the same process that has formed you so far, you can form yourself from now on, a step and a choice at a time.

For my part, I *do* believe that I have come to this world for a mission—for some reason, for some specific reason. I am on this earth for a reason. And that doesn't mean that I have to bring peace to the Middle East—although I yearn to do so. I don't have to be Madame Curie. Or Albert Schweitzer. But I *can* do certain things to touch certain people on this earth—in this life, my life. I can make myself grow in such a way that it affects both me and others. I am worthwhile. And so, I believe, are you.

Many of us, unless we're famous, discount the importance of what's happening in our worlds. And that—to me—is another way of diminishing ourselves. Suppose Thomas Edison had listened to people who thought he was just a crazy inventor for experimenting with five hundred filament materials before he found the carbon filament that would keep his light bulb burning—and light up the world. Suppose Dr. William Thomas Morton had listened when the entire medical profession laughed long and hard about his experiments with ether for anesthesia. What will be lost if *you* let somebody nibble away at *your* attempts to grow?

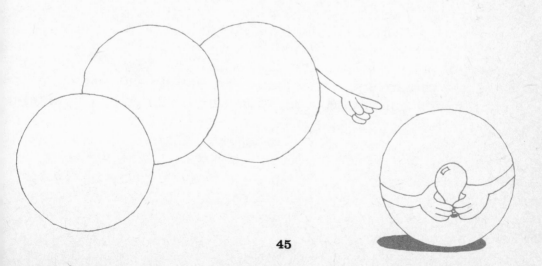

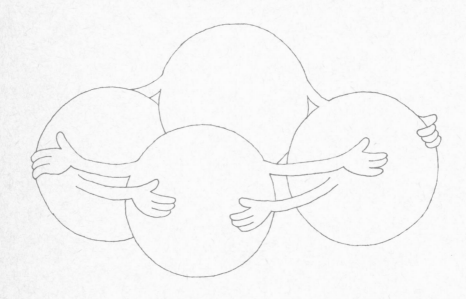

It's part of the great paradox that when you discover that Self —your kernel—you are also likely then to know fully why you're here, how you fit in, how you're part of the great universal human community.

How to Find Your Kernel of Power

How to *find* your kernel of power? The process, as I've said, is simple—but it's not easy.

We are all apt to forget our strengths and the power we have at our core when we are in situations that are either new or stressful.

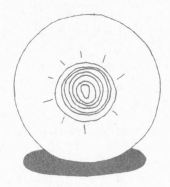

So discovering what is constant—your kernel of power—is your way to stay centered and at your best.

Doing real self-empowerment *for* yourself is *very* different from identifying skills and merely building self-esteem. Many people have thought about their skills. People who have done such thinking do have self-esteem and feel better about themselves—perhaps for six months or more.

The process *we* are about to begin is a deeper process, and its effects should last a lifetime and never desert you.

Once you have found your kernel, when the moment comes that you know you lack the skills in a situation, you can quickly recenter yourself with the certainty of the strengths you possess.

The empowerment process is as simple as asking yourself some questions. But it's hard to do, because you have to delve deeply inside yourself.

It's also frightening. "What if there's nothing there? Or what if I'm not, after all, very good? Or worth very much? What if I'm as inconsequential as I've been treating myself?" You're not. Nobody is inconsequential.

You'd be surprised how many people don't know their strengths, have never thought about them. But they are—in sum—you. That's worth discovering. That's even worth some discomfort and some hard work, isn't it? Because only you can do it. Nobody else can.

But help with that process is a delicate matter. Well-meaning people can short-circuit the process for others by trying to do the task of self-empowerment *for* them. But note that the word is *self*-empowerment. It starts from inside out. It does not *work* from outside in.

Compliments from others *feel* good. But they don't last.

Some compliments are an attempt to boost somebody's feelings about himself or herself.

You must do the empowering for yourself. Compliments help only after you have done the work.

That kernel, that central part of you, that self, is your source of joy and serenity. And balance and respect and competence and stability. And power.

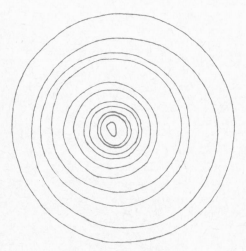

SELF-EMPOWERMENT:
YOU ARE THE ONLY ONE
YOU WILL EVER HAVE.
YOU HAVE EVERYTHING
YOU NEED INSIDE YOU.

It's your abiding strength—a source nobody can touch or harm. You have to find it. And then you will carry it wherever you go.

Another question—perhaps the most important one—is: What happens to you if you *don't* find your kernel? What if you choose never to look? Do you have a choice not to grow—not to search?

As Langston Hughes says in his poem, "Harlem":

> What happens to a dream deferred?
> Does it dry up like a raisin in the sun? . . .
> Maybe it just sags like a heavy load.
> Or does it explode?

Every day you meet people who have dried up like a raisin in the sun. Every day you meet people who have deferred their dreams and have no sense of urgency.

Sometimes people explode, in mid life, when the stakes are high, and time seems limited. You can wait until there is a crisis. But you don't have to. You can start today to discover what is at your core.

I know a man who came on the earth equipped with brains, good health, good looks, plentiful material resources. By all society's material standards he would be accounted a success. But he only uses a quarter of what he's capable of. He has the potential to be creative but plays it safe in his job and his life, living on the warmed-over ideas of others. The only spark in his life is his young daughter. What he says he wants her to be is an independent, creative thinker. And every day what he models for her is the opposite. He has been throughout his life too careful to avoid the perilous but exciting journey to the core of his self.

So, how to find your kernel? Here is the outline for the process. You will have to pay close attention to your Self as you work through the process—to make yourself push deeper, work harder, think more carefully than you have ever done before.

Begin by asking yourself this question:

● What is it about me that is unique?

Remember that unique means "one." What is there about you that is special, that nobody else can bring to this world? That's no ordinary question. It's hard. It may seem unanswerable. Or it may take many years to answer.

There is a difference between a strength and a skill. A strength is something you are born with, something from the center of yourself. A skill is something you have learned to do.

We all have both strengths and skills. What we want to find are the strengths. They lead to finding your kernel. Your skills will turn out to be clues to your kernel. Don't think that your skills are your kernel.

Most people tie their feelings of self-confidence and self-worth to their skills. Then, when new skills are required, they are suddenly at sea. What they need to do is to realize that their power and confidence are strengths drawn from the core of themselves—that hard-won self-knowledge that is a never-diminished source of life and personal power. That life-giving, self-renewing power goes everywhere with you—into every situation, every environment.

What makes some people exciting, what makes people leaders, what makes them charismatic? How does one person excite others and inspire them to do things, dare things they would never dare on their own? Energy and imagination are certainly part of it, but where does that energy come from? Why does an orchestra play competently with one conductor, but play an inspired, exciting performance with another? It's not just that one is a bad musician, the other a good one. It has something to do with an energy, and an ability to call out and encourage risk in others. Why do students achieve with one teacher and not with another? Where does that energy come from? I believe it comes from people who are operating out of their kernel, who have got into touch with the very center of their being.

Go slowly. When images come into your mind that *seem* unrelated, don't ignore them. Follow them. They will guide you toward self-understanding.

Every piece of life is, I believe, significant. And this extends to jokes, slips of the tongue, light comments that are gone before they are realized. Listen, even to jokes, perhaps especially to jokes. Sometimes they contain bitter information that can't be comfortably surfaced in any other way. Sometimes they are a way a person uses to diminish herself or himself. Sometimes they are a cry for help.

Once a man I worked with in a group followed up my presentation on "boundaries" by calling them "barriers." When we talked about that, he realized that he had surfaced some important information about his behaviors, and he learned from it. Sometimes self-deprecating jokes are a habit. By doing this—and without meaning to—people make themselves into smaller circles. A friend of mine who considers herself awkward says that she is "a high-risk walker." She says that walls reach out and strike her, steps jump up and trip her. In every slip or light comment, there is a grain of truth. We can either let those pass or see them as signs to guide us toward further exploration.

Begin by listing your strengths.

One person I worked with said:

- "I'm a pretty good writer."
- "I'm a fairly good cook."
- "I'm curious—a learning freak."

"Would you say that without qualifiers?" I asked her. "Be uncensored. Be as celebratory of yourself as you can. I know *I'm* not finished in my growth process. And neither are you. You won't *always* be generous, or kind, or thoughtful or considerate. The sun doesn't *always* shine. Sometimes it's hidden behind clouds. But the sun is *there.* It comes up every day. *Your* unique qualities are there, even if they're not always apparent in your behavior."

"Okay. [Doubtfully] I'm a good writer. I'm a good cook. I'm curious. I like to learn."

"Cooking is a skill. It's something you've learned. We want to list strengths—those special talents you were born with, ways in which you're special."

"Okay. I like to be helpful to other people. I have—I think—a sense of humor. I—find the world funny. Sometimes that's not appreciated—the 'long cosmic view,' I call it."

"What's that—the long cosmic view?"

"Well—if you step back and look at most things in terms of the entire cosmos and the full span of time—they're fairly insignificant. So I find most kinds of human antics—often my own included—pretty funny. And even things that seem tragic in human terms probably aren't very in the long cosmic view."

"Could you say more about that?

How does that suggest your core—your kernel?

Does it suggest your kernel?"

"I think it does. Connected to my view of the world is a theory I have about living."

"What's that?"

"If you look at death—at the physical facts of death and decay—it's pretty gruesome. And part of the fear of death is that knowledge—knowing in your bones that it's coming.

"My parents died when I was young, so I've thought about this a good deal. Thinking about what death does—to everybody—seems to me somehow necessary if I want to find the sense to this life. Death comes to us all and certainly may negate everything we've tried to do in our lives. So, you could say, what's the use of doing anything—really?

"You could look at this world—it's often evil as well as good—and decide to give up. But something keeps me from doing that."

"What's that?"

"I don't know. It's curious. It's almost as if once I decide there's no good reason to keep on acting in ways I believe are right—because I'm going to die anyway—I decide it's important to live—for the reason of life. It's important to live and act in the short time we all have. Something affirmative, some life comes up in me.

"I think it's important to do it well. But I'm afraid I'm very far afield."

"I don't think so. What do you think is at your core that has to do with what you've told me?"

"My feeling that life is for living—well, with honor and compassion and courage—because by doing it that way you invest it with meaning—no matter what you believe happens after death. That—and my respect for the toughness and vigor of life—its recurrence. I admire toughness of spirit and the will to live—that perennial quality of grass and the human spirit. I believe that we must affirm life again and again—even in the face of death."

"Is that at your core?"

"I think—probably—that's my kernel."

By now, my friend was in tears, almost unable to speak her last point steadily. It nearly *always* happens, I point out—that when a person begins to talk about the core itself, tears come.

"And you?"

"Me? Well, if I were to go through the process and list my strengths, I would say that I see myself as persistent. And, I have a lot of energy. And I take risks. I'm a risk-taker."

"How do *those* things go together? Where do they lead?"

"Well, let's see. My risk-taking has to do with my feelings about missed opportunities. I'm afraid not to do something for fear I'll never have the opportunity again."

"Why is that?"

"My feelings about not having a chance again are connected with my feelings about death—because I've explored my feelings about my own death. I've done a lot of thinking about death. I hope to get another chance on the earth, but in case I don't, I want to make sure that I grow as much as I can in this life."

"Yes, well how does that connect with your kernel?"

"Let's see. We started the list with 'persistence.' How do I play that out? I think I play out my persistence with the energy I put into things. My risk-taking is connected with the feeling that I may not have this opportunity again. And that's connected with my feeling about death and life. *That's* connected to my feeling that I want to grow myself as much as I can. And *that's* connected with my wish to encourage other people to grow."

"So if I ask you what you're here on earth for?"

"I want to grow myself as much as I can, but I believe I'm here to help others fall in love with themselves so they will want to grow themselves as much as *they* can. I'm talking about the self-acceptance a person needs to have to be able to put aside self-criticism long enough to find the strength at their core. Then once that is found, they will be able to grow other parts of themselves with new-found energy and vitality.

"And if I ask myself what it is that is unique about me, what there is that, if I told a friend, the friend would say, 'Yes, that's right,' it's that I bring my joy about living with me. I'm able to communicate my excitement about life. And then I'm able to affect other people. I can walk into *any* situation, and people feel my excitement about living. They feel my joy."

"That's your core, your kernel?"

"Yes, I believe that what's at my core is my intense joy in living. My joy in life is my kernel of power."

"I'm not sure I see how this relates to self-empowerment."

"My feeling about life—about how short it is and how precious—affects everything I do. I have no time to be afraid of looking foolish. I have things to do—and a limited time to do them. I have to make every minute count. When I get up in the morning, I say: 'Thank God, I'm alive today.' And that energy sparks people I work with. You see, the important thing about finding out what your unique strength is, is that it provides a center, a foundation for the rest of you. You need no longer compare yourself with anybody, because who you are doesn't depend on your skills, or your experience, or what you know or whom you know."

"You know, that sounds a lot like *my* kernel."

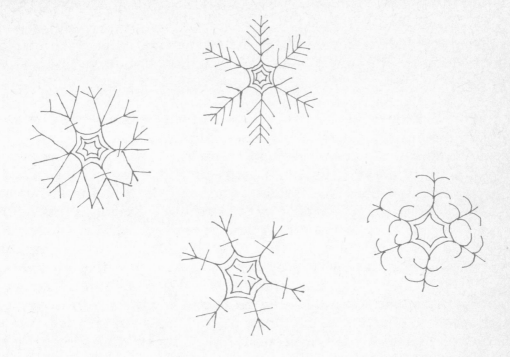

"Yes, I suppose it does. But how we play out our strength is different. *My* kernel makes me both different from everybody else, and in some sense the same, part of the same human wish to grow that drives every living, growing thing. Once you know yourself, you can recognize that you are valuable to a group and to the world in a way nobody else could possibly be. You are as particular as a wildflower or a snowflake. Snowflakes are all just water; it's how the crystals arrange themselves that makes each snowflake special and beautiful."

Once you have tapped into your source of power—the deep and abiding values that fill your being, you can pursue any occupation that your strengths and skills lead you to. Any honest occupation has value in the world, so long as, for you, it is not in conflict with your core, your kernel.

We don't all grow in the same ways—or at the same rates. I usually grow in a direct way, with full awareness of what I am trying to do. But one person that I know and love and respect grows in less direct ways —in community service, in expanding himself artistically (through guitar lessons and Spanish lessons). Another friend has used her expert skills at bridge in all sorts of ways to grow. As she plays that game, she uses one of her kernel strengths—analytical thinking. She also teaches the game to elderly people. That permits her to use another strength from her kernel—a deep respect and caring for others. She says the game itself is less important for these people than the achievement and the experience of feeling respected for their own analytical competence and ability to learn a new skill. She also uses it as a way to include newcomers in the community. For those who already play bridge, she uses the game as a way for them to connect with others easily using a familiar skill. She is growing herself as she does these things and because they come from her kernel, people can sense it. And once you understand what your source of personal renewal is, you will see that the drive to have *more* personal power simply expresses your innermost need to be the best that you can be.

Being the biggest circle you can be is simply your drive to make the most of your life. Being the biggest circle you can be is a sacred responsibility.

There is no instant formula. This is a process that works from the inside out. What I offer you is not free from conflict. And it's not my goal to make people comfortable. I *do* want to offer the kind of challenge that produces growth. That may bring with it temporary discomfort.

You should pay attention to the people who encourage you to grow. These are not always the people who coddle you, not always the people who seem to wish to protect you. Protection is sometimes a form of limitation.

Relationships—of all kinds—are like sand held in your hand. Held loosely, with an open hand, the sand remains where it is. The minute you close your hand and squeeze tightly to hold on, the sand trickles through your fingers. You may hold on to some of it, but most will be spilled. A relationship is like that. Held loosely, with respect and freedom for the other person, it is likely to remain intact. But hold too tightly, too possessively, and the relationship slips away and is lost.

This is equally true of relationships between lovers—parents and children—teachers and students—and friends. Everyone needs space and freedom to grow.

People who offer you conflict may be offering you the opportunity for growth. Seek such people out. These are the people who can show you that you *can* do it for yourself. You *can* be a big circle.

To review, this is the process:

1. List your strengths. Remember, those are things you're born with, not things you've learned.

2. Now look at your list. Take out any skills that may have got in there. Leave out qualifiers.

3. Look at your list of strengths. Ask yourself:

    ● Why is that important to me?
    ● What's underneath that reason?
       Answer: I want to do something.

Ask yourself: What makes me want to *do* that?

Why?

- How are your strengths tied to each other?
- What is at your center?
- What do you have that you take with you everywhere?

If you get stuck and want to try another direction:

- What are you here on earth for?
- What did you come to do?

Think of the things you do in life that

- are important to you
- make you feel a sense of joy

Now take those things, and ask the questions you've just asked again.

- Why is this important to you?
- How is it tied to your strength?
- What is your kernel?

Being the Biggest Circle You Can Be

With others, you can behave *as if* they were already the bigger circles they want to be. Don't suppose that they don't want to be bigger. What you now know is that nearly everybody *wants* to be bigger. You may be the person who will challenge them to *become* bigger. Like you, they will "become" the person they are treated like. Everybody has seen what happens when an ordinary person takes on a title or an office. When a new President is inaugurated, he takes on the awe and respect of his office and begins to act like—the President. Ordinary men (and I would certainly hope, one day, ordinary women)—haberdashers, country lawyers, former movie actors—lose their old roles and *become* the President. A person who acts "as if" soon "is." Someone once said: "We become what we pretend to be; so we must be very careful what we pretend to be."

What I say to you is this. What I offer you is not without risk. You could get nibbled. But you know how to handle that now. You could make somebody mad at you. But now you know that you can handle that by quietly insisting on your right to grow.

You could misuse your own power as a big circle. But now you know that truly big circles don't have to be center stage all the time.

To have someone else grow to be a big circle doesn't diminish you as a big circle. So now you can handle that threat.

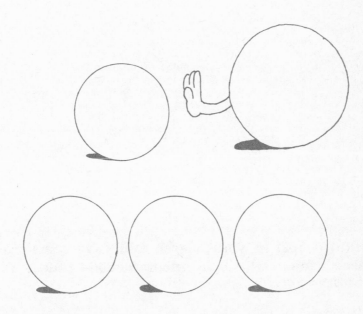

You could get lost in your search and have some trouble finding your way back. You could have uncomfortable times. You could feel foolish.

Or you could have a fine adventure. But where you're going to arrive is worth it all. Whom you are going to discover when you're there is worth it.

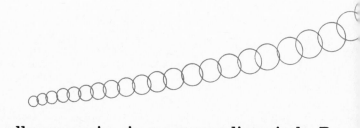

Now it's time to begin all over again—in a never-ending circle. Because circles can continue to grow.

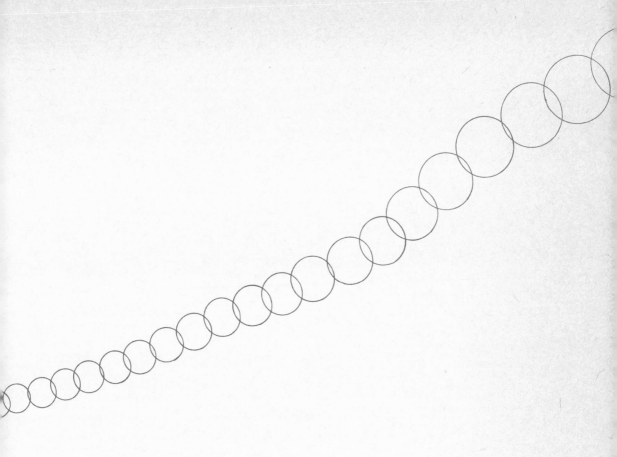

You can grow even more. For as long as life lasts, no circle can ever be big enough.

**Nothing ventured,
something lost.***

Neale Clapp

74